AF426170

ZY'RIELLE'S
BRACELET

ISBN 979-8-88851-493-1 (Paperback)
ISBN 979-8-88851-494-8 (Digital)

Copyright © 2024 Marissa Smith
All rights reserved
First Edition

All rights reserved. No part of this publication may be reproduced, distributed, or transmitted in any form or by any means, including photocopying, recording, or other electronic or mechanical methods without the prior written permission of the publisher. For permission requests, solicit the publisher via the address below.

Covenant Books
11661 Hwy 707
Murrells Inlet, SC 29576
www.covenantbooks.com

ZY'RIELLE'S
BRACELET

Marissa Smith

Zy'rielle is a girl with many different talents. She can sing and dance and is good at making friends. One thing she isn't good at is math. Zy'rielle was failing her math class, and there was one more test before school ended for the year. She knew she had to find a way to pass so she could go to summer camp with the rest of her friends. She knew that her mom wouldn't let her go if she didn't pass.

"What am I going to do?" Zy'rielle said as she heard the news from Ms. Jackson, her math teacher.

"You are going to have to study, Zy'rielle," Ms. Jackson said.

"Oh great!" said Zy'rielle. "Now I have to break this news to my mom."

Zy'rielle began to feel butterflies as the bus approaching her house stopped. She sighed and got off the bus.

As she rang the doorbell, she could hear her mom in the house listening to music so she knew she was in a good mood. Zy'rielle thought to herself, *Maybe she won't be upset about my math grade.*

Mom would always be in a good mood when music plays. Mom answered the door with a big smile. "Hello there, little beauty. Come in and take off your school clothes, and do you have homework?" Mom said.

Zy'rielle stopped in her tracks thinking about that math grade she just got from Ms. Jackson. "No, ma'am. I don't have homework," she said with a look of guilt on her face. Mom noticed the response wasn't the normal response from Zy'rielle so she asked what was wrong. Zy'rielle turned with tears in her eyes, "Mom, I am failing math." Zy'rielle ran to her mom for comfort. "What am I going to do? I can't go to summer camp."

Mom looked at her and said, "Wipe your tears, and go get your math book so we can study."

Zy'rielle and Mom went over problem after problem to ensure she had them correct. Zy'rielle was getting all the questions right. She was comfortable learning with her mom and knew she wasn't as confident at passing without Mom there.

"I wish you could be there with me, Mom."

Mom looked and replied, "I can't go to school with you, Zy'rielle. You know that."

Zy'rielle began to cry. "I'm comfortable with you being there with me, Mom," she said.

Mom looked upon Zy'rielle as she sat at the table with tears in her eyes and thought to herself, *There has to be something I can do to fix this.*

Mom went into her room and grabbed a bracelet from her jewelry box. It was her favorite bracelet, which she had gotten for her birthday a few years ago. Mom knew Zy'rielle also liked the bracelet as well.

"This should comfort her while she is taking her test," Mom said. Mom ran out of the room and told Zy'rielle she had a solution to her problem. Mom placed the bracelet on Zy'rielle and told her she could wear it on testing day. "It'll be like I'm right there with you."

Zy'rielle smiled and ran into the room to prepare for dinnertime.

The next morning, Zy'rielle jumped out of bed and got dressed for school. "Today is my math test," she said while putting on her shoes. She grabbed her backpack and went off to the bus stop.

As she got off the bus and entered school, Zy'rielle was well-prepared for her math test. As she sat at her desk, Ms. Jackson began handing out test papers to all the students in her class. Ms. Jackson told everyone they had thirty minutes to complete the test and set her timer.

"You may begin," Ms. Jackson said as she set the timer on her desk. Zy'rielle wrote her name on the top of the paper and glanced at the test. Butterflies began to fill her stomach with nervousness like before.

"I can do this!" Zy'rielle said looking at her mom's bracelet. Zy'rielle finished her test and handed her test to Ms. Jackson.

"Sit quietly until all the other students have completed the test, and then I will grade you."

"Yes, ma'am," said Zy'rielle as she sat back in her seat. Zy'rielle sat anxiously, eager to know what her grade would be. Ms. Jackson graded the test and began passing them back to all the students, flipped over.

Ms. Jackson told the students not to flip the test papers until everyone had their test back, so everyone could see their grades together.

Ms. Jackson counted down, "Five, four, three, two, one. Flip your test papers."

Zy'rielle flipped her test and couldn't believe her grade. It was a big A+ on the top of her paper. Zy'rielle shouted with excitement, "I did it! I can go to summer camp!" Zy'rielle placed the test paper in her backpack so she could show Mom her passing grade.

The bell rang, and Zy'rielle ran to the bus to go home. As the bus approached its stop, she jumped off the bus. She ran as fast as she could until she made it home and rang the doorbell.

Mom answered the door with a smile on her face.

"Mom, I did it! I passed my math test." She pulled the test out of her backpack and showed Mom her grade.

"Now, I can go pack for summer camp."
Mom laughed and said, "Yes, you can go to summer camp."
As Zy'rielle walked into her room and began to pack her bag for summer camp, she realized the bracelet was all the comfort she needed.

About the Author

Marissa is an amazing mother that also once struggled in math. Marissa knows how important education is and encourages children to do their very best no matter how challenging it may be. However, Marissa thinks she has come up with a brilliant idea that could change the way children look at taking tests.

www.ingramcontent.com/pod-product-compliance
Lightning Source LLC
Chambersburg PA
CBHW040159110726
48005CB00018B/2831